KNOWLEDGE PUBLICATIONS

Andrea del Sarto

ROBIN IRONSIDE

Andrea del Sarto 1486-1530

Andrea del Sarto, the son of Agnolo, a tailor, was born in Florence on 16 July 1486. He remained there all his life except for a few months spent in France during 1518-19, and perhaps a brief visit to Rome, although there are no documents to prove this. We owe almost all we know about his life to the contemporary art historian, Vasari, who knew him personally, and for a time was an assistant in his studio.

According to Vasari, Andrea was sent when he was seven to train under a goldsmith. Later he is recorded as working under a certain Gian Barile, a Florentine painter of crude, large-scale works. When Barile saw the boy's rapid progress he had him apprenticed to Piero di Cosimo, with whom he stayed for several years, until, tired of the caprices of his eccentric master, he formed a partnership with Franciabigio. When he entered the artists' guild of St. Luke in 1508 he was sharing a room with him in the Piazza del Grano.

As well as Vasari's account in 'Lives of the Painters', there are a certain number of documents recording payments for his work, and dates attached to some of his works, which help to identify the main landmarks of his career, regrettably cut short.

Rome is generally considered to have taken the lead in all forms of art during the formative years of his life, but in fact Florence had been stirred into action by the revolutionary works left there during the opening years of the sixteenth century by Leonardo, Michelangelo and Raphael. Andrea was considered to be one of the leading artists in Florence of his day, a fact substantiated by the invitation he received to go to France as Court Painter to Francis I, and by his flourishing workshop and extensive commissions. However, from the long passage devoted to him in Vasari's 'Lives', there emerges a pathetic picture of a gentle, modest and far too submissive man who allowed himself to be ruined both socially and materially by his excessive attachment to his apparently tyrannical and self-centred wife, Lucrezia del Fede, whom he married in 1517. It was supposedly through her persuasions that the painter broke his promise to return to France, thus incurring the anger of Francis I. Vasari also gives frequent indications that Andrea lived under constant financial stress because he had to abandon his own relations in dire straits in order to support those of his wife, although he had a constant income from the great demand for his work. He also gives an account of his lonely death while his wife refused to come near him in terror of the plague, and there are tales of her shrewish and violent behaviour towards his pupils.

Perhaps Vasari retained a vivid memory of some unhappy experience in Andrea's workshop and tried thus to vindicate himself years later by this malicious image of Lucrezia, who was still alive. But his fabrication of the artist's shabby and retiring life may also be explained by an inherent tendency in his work to relate the circumstances of an artist's life to his pictorial style. Apart from his obvious bitterness towards Lucrezia it may have been an attempt to explain a certain lack of creative energy which he felt in Andrea's work. It is important to remember that in other passages of his work, when he records him among his companions of the Compagnia del Paiuolo (the Kettle), or mixing with the other members of the Compagnia della Cazzuola (the Trowel). These were evidently brilliant gatherings of friends of some common interest or charitable intent, who took it in turns to sponsor the dinner and provide for it some extravagant, and often macabre, culinary spectacle. One given by Andrea is described: 'Andrea del Sarto presented an eight-sided temple like that of San Giovanni (the Baptistry of Florence), but with columns above. The floor was a great platter of jelly in coloured sections like mosaic. The columns which seemed made of porphyry were tall, thick salami sausages, the bases and capitals formed from Parmesan cheese. The cornice was of sweetmeats, and the tribunal built of squares of marzipan. In the middle a music-stand had been constructed from cold veal, holding a book of lasagna with the letters and notes picked out in pepper corns. The singers were roast thrushes held upright, their beaks open and wearing surplices of thin strips of pork. Behind them were two fat pigeons as the bases, and six garden warblers as trebles.'

When all this is taken into account, Andrea could not have been quite as poverty stricken as Vasari would have us think. His misfortunes, of whatever stature, must have originated primarily from his careless and disorganised way of life.

He died in Florence in January 1531, probably of the plague rather than 'an orgy of eating', after the stringent conditions imposed by the Siege of Florence of the previous year.

'Andrea del Sarto — the faultless painter' — ROBERT BROWNING

Andrea del Sarto was a younger contemporary of Leonardo da Vinci, Michelangelo and Raphael, a circumstance which, by itself, supplies important information about the character of his art. The example of these three great painters both solicited and compelled admiration and their genius affected the whole complexion of Italian art. Painters of their own and of succeeding generations were spellbound by their mastery, and nowhere with more subjection than in Tuscany of which Leonardo and Michelangelo were natives, and where Raphael's brilliance first received that astonished notice which his subsequent achievements regularly attracted.

ANDREA DEL SARTO was born in Florence in 1486; Leonardo was then thirty-four; Michelangelo was eleven and Raphael was three years old. Irresistible as their influence proved to be, the magnitude of their success must have discouraged any hope of surpassing it. This frustrating situation had an unnerving effect upon the more vigorous personalities among their successors of the Mannerist School, whose art may be fruitfully expounded as a neurotic evasion of an influence which may have seemed, perhaps, to threaten their identity. Andrea was not a Mannerist; as a close contemporary of Michelangelo and Raphael, his artistic personality was engulfed rather than unbalanced by their example. Vasari states that as a painter his besetting weakness was a certain timidity of spirit. The authority of genius had intimidated stronger minds than his. It was not only, however, in this understandable respect that Andrea's painting seems to have been impaired by an element of pusillanimity in his character. That veneration for the re-discovered culture of classical antiquity which was the most significant single feature of the Renaissance had reached a point, as far as the visual arts were concerned, at which the standards of the Greeks and Romans were regarded as canonical; the art of antiquity as it was increasingly brought to light by the excavation of Hellenistic sculpture appeared to reveal a perfection which Raphael and Michelangelo were pleased to acknowledge. Even the dress of the period followed this pervasive classicism and the elegant extravagance of quattrocento clothes was replaced by a sober draped style which tended to inflate the natural silhouette and produced a statuesque appearance consonant with classical taste. Painters were expected to supply pictures in accordance with the current ideals of classical antiquity; and the age of academies was in sight.

Andrea del Sarto was fully equipped to reward this expectation. He did so with a correctness and virtuosity which was at once applauded, but it was seen that his compositions, often, it was agreed, faultlessly executed, lacked conceptual vigour. His classicism was marked by an emotional hesitancy to which critics today are no less sensitive than Vasari. It should in fairness be said, however, that Andrea's art produced what the taste of the day was hostile to, the spontaneous expansion of his artistic temperament. There is no evidence to show whether or not Andrea was a man of any considerable education: but the ideas and ideals of the Renaissance were, of course, the exclusive property of an educated minority; the social status of artists was still such that we can say no more of them in this connection than that they might, or might not, have been persons of general culture and thus likely to have understood and endorsed the classical humanism of the cultured minority. In Florence, the ascendancy of Savonarola, who perished at the stake when Andrea was twelve years old, had demonstrated that the submerged masses, on whom the friar relied for his support, retained unchanged the beliefs and mental attitudes of the Middle Ages. It is not fanciful to suppose that Andrea's somewhat insipid acceptance of the classicism of the High Renaissance may have been partly due to an untutored understanding.

TODAY, Andrea's art is not, on the whole, esteemed as it deserves and until the publication in the present decade of Freedberg's and Shearman's comprehensive studies it evoked no considerable interest among the majority of persons interested in painting. The irreproachable correctness of his performance, so greatly admired in the past, is now an anachronistic merit. His moderate reputation in our time, however, might be chiefly ascribed to the unpalatable sentimentality of his rendering of facial expression.

3

1. STUDY FOR AN APOSTLE. UFFIZI, FLORENCE

The capacity to portray, with convincing naturalism, the quality of an emotion or mood, as far as these are perceptible in a person's features, constituted at the beginning of the sixteenth century a technical advance in the science of representation; it was an aim to which, since Giotto, Italian painters had given consistent and, in their view, perhaps exclusive attention. Any progress in this respect was acclaimed, and the professional skill with which Andrea could delineate the expressions of the face was enthusiastically approved by his own and many subsequent generations.

Today we no longer regard the successful imitation of natural appearances as an adequate or suitable means of aesthetic expression. Even in the productions of Leonardo, who was the first to perfect the portrayal of facial expression, that recurring mysterious smile is saved perhaps only by its weirdness from affecting us unpleasantly. Andrea's naturalism is more pronounced, and the depiction of grief, for example, on the Virgin's face in his *Pietà* (Plate XIII) or of adoration on that of the infant Christ in *The Virgin and Child with St. John* (Plate V) seems obtrusive to the modern eye.

But the present decline in Andrea's reputation is of relatively recent origin. His posthumous fame was maintained with fluctuations until the nineteenth century, during which, in one sense, it may be said to have increased. His sentimental naturalism appealed to the Romantic imagination and a legend grew up around his name, echoes of which were still heard at the beginning of our century, though there cannot today be many people to whom it is familiar.

The legend arose on the slender foundation of a short passage in Vasari's life of the painter, in which the biographer sketches a depressing picture of Andrea's relations with his wife, Lucrezia, whose character is presented to the reader in a most unflattering light. Out of this was formed an image of Lucrezia as a beautiful woman in whose charms the sensitive Andrea was helplessly enthralled and who supported her voracious family, and even her lovers, on the profits of his genius. Such is the general character of the legend of which, among the various forms in which it was retailed, the most notable versions are the poem by Browning and the play by de Musset. How much truth it contained cannot be determined. Vasari, however, was in a position to know the truth even if he did not tell it; and there is nothing in the ascertainable facts to refute his view of the painter's domestic situation. Unfortunately, however, these facts are few, and a study of the progress of Andrea's painting is unsupported by any adequate knowledge of his other activities.

AT THE AGE of twelve in 1498 he was apprenticed to Piero di Cosimo, with whom he remained until 1508, in which year he is known to have been established as an independent painter. The character of his mature style would hardly suggest that he had at any time studied under the guidance of Piero. But the latter's influence is apparent in the most considerable of Andrea's earlier productions, the frescoes illustrating the life of S. Filippo Benizzi in the church of SS. Annunziata at Florence. It is revealed, notably in the painting of *The Punishment of the Gamblers* (Plates II and III) in the marked diffusion of emphases throughout the composition, in the somewhat fortuitous disposition of the figures and in the fanciful accidents of the landscape background. These frescoes are the work of an artist of talent and feeling. But they are immature; they aspire, in parts, towards that breadth of treatment approved by the classicism of the age, but the resulting effect is one of self-conscious simplicity, amounting uneasily at times to a Giottesque economy of statement.

A less demanding work, probably painted soon afterwards, demonstrates the ease and rapidity of Andrea's approach to the classical manner. This is the *Tobias Altar* (Kunsthistorisches Museum, Vienna), which in the harmonious design, the rhythmic, ample flow of the draperies and the absence of any local accessories must have made it seem to current taste an entirely unexceptionable work. It is also significant as perhaps the earliest confident, if imperfect, revelation of that smooth and dexterous handling and that melting tenderness of feeling on which his subsequent fame was largely founded. Indeed, the smoothness and sweetness he exhibits here are excessive and the work is an emphatic if unfair illustration of the characteristics which have tended to depress his reputation today.

At about the same time as this picture was painted (c. 1511), Andrea was entrusted with the execution of a further work in SS. Annunziata, *The Procession of the Magi* (Plate IV), and in 1513-14 he was engaged on *The Birth of the Virgin* (Plate VI-VII) for the same church. Both works are in the exacting medium of fresco and altogether more ambitious in scope than the *Tobias Altar*. They have been greatly praised, especially the later painting, and they unquestionably display a degree of maturity lacking in the earlier frescoed scenes from the life of S. Filippo Benizzi. But the current classical ideal which the artist here clearly strove to satisfy has not been more than fragmentarily approached; it has been sought with greater understanding than in the earlier frescoes, but with less success than in the comparatively simple problem presented by the *Tobias Altar*. The latter picture is, of course, immensely inferior as a work of art to the later Annunziata frescoes, but the superiority of these is due to their vivid possession of the qualities which are typical of the art of the previous century; they are alive with local colour and enriched with contemporary detail, thus frustrating any generalization of the subject matter such as classicism demanded.

Of *The Birth of the Virgin* it has been justly said that this is a social document of contemporary Florentine society, 'a record of a visit of congratulation to a wealthy house in which an heiress has been born'. The two visitors, in the foreground of the composition, are made conspicuous by the studied amplitude of their proportions; they are deliberately cast in the classic mode. But their ponderous dignity looks unduly contrived and at once confirms the assumption that Andrea accepted classicism, however unconsciously, with uneasy reserves. The same response is as readily evoked by the absurdly overdraped figure in the left foreground of *The Procession of the Magi*. But, though Andrea's art as a whole suggests that he was neither emotionally nor intellectually in sympathy with classicism, few of his subsequent works show less than a mastery of its outward forms.

The Virgin and Child with St. John, painted in about 1516, illustrates the high degree of what, if we compare it with the *Tobias Altar*, we may fairly call the professional sophistication with which Andrea learnt to handle the classical manner. It is perhaps the first entirely successful work in his long series of Madonnas, Holy Families and other sacred groups, most of which are distinguished by studied design, sweetness of expression and generalized interpretation. If, as Freedberg believes, the recurring features of a model for the Madonna among these works were in fact taken from the painter's wife, there is nothing humanly improbable in the legend that he was at the mercy of her charms notwithstanding the vices of her character.

BY THE END of the first decade of the sixteenth century the rival states, of which Italy for centuries had been comprised, had little prospect of preserving real independence for much longer. Attempts to infuse a spirit of nationality strong enough to consume their internecine differences had met with small success; the peninsula was now the coveted prey of the rising French and Spanish monarchies, and the conflict between them for the largest share of the prize dominated Italian politics for the next twenty years.

Florence, although it had been restored to Medicean rule by Spanish power in 1512, was francophil by tradition and commercial interest. This link was strengthened, in the cultural sphere, by the accession to the French throne of Francis I, a patron of the arts, who attached Leonardo da Vinci to his court in 1516 and summoned Andrea to France in 1518. Andrea was back in Florence before the end of the following year and remained in Tuscany until his death. Vasari declares that he was unable to resist Lucrezia's importunate demands for his presence in Florence but that he had been authorized to make a temporary visit only and dishonoured an obligation by failing to return. There is no reason to disbelieve his biographer; nor, however, is there any reason to interpret this incident as evidence that his relations with his wife must have been more amicable than Vasari elsewhere asserts; the fatal attractions of her person might have sufficed to lure him to Italy.

To what extent Andrea's brief stay at Fontainebleau may have exerted an effect on French painting cannot be estimated with any certainty. But it is worth noting, and not only in this connection, that where Andrea's subject-matter, or some detail of it, has the character of a genre subject he displays a peculiar gift for endowing apparently accidental groups of figures with an aesthetic grace that might be more closely described as lyrical; and something of this quality is to be found in the pastoral treatment of genre subjects by the painters of the Fontainebleau school.

In Andrea's art this manner derived probably from his training in the outlook and procedures of an outmoded

2. STUDY FOR A NUDE. LOUVRE, PARIS

generation; it is well illustrated in the little scenes which compose the two pictures of *Stories from the Life of Joseph* (Plate X-XI) and in the rustic figures of the background to the Louvre *Charity* (Fig. 3) which is known to have been painted in France; however, it is perhaps revealed most beautifully in the disposition of the subsidiary figures in *The Visitation* of the Scalzo Cloister in Florence.

THE DECORATION of the courtyard of the Confraternity of the Scalzo is the masterpiece of Andrea's career. He worked upon it intermittently from c. 1511 until 1526. The merits of the successive compositions narrating the life of St. John the Baptist which he painted on the walls of the courtyard improved steadily as time passed. In the later examples, the painter's highly developed talent for naturalistic representation—and perhaps also the dramatic character of the subject—seems to have over-

come the exigencies of the classical manner and there is an unadorned grace and vigour in *The Christening* and *The Beheading;* qualities of his art which the apparatus of classical design in, for example, *The Sacrifice of Isaac* (Plate XVI) effectively conceals. However, the Scalzo paintings are, for the most part, relieved of that air of constraint which is apparent in Andrea's art when it is harnessed to the pictorial conventions of the High Renaissance, and this because they were evidently conceived as the components of, in the most modern sense, a scheme of decoration. Admirable as many of them are judged as self-sufficient works, the lasting impression on the spectator is one of most harmonious and elegant decoration, beautifully adapted to the architecture for which it was devised. The painting is in 'grisaille', embodying a remarkable tonal variety rising to a pale, yellowish note, but since the setting is rectangular, no real idea of the over-all effect can be conveyed by reproduction.

Large-scale wall-painting at the beginning of the sixteenth century took little account of decorative problems. The wall paintings of Michelangelo, Titian and Raphael are monumental in character; they overpower rather than embellish the buildings in which they are to be found. In the case of the artists quoted this result is largely due to the force of genius. But, in general, lesser painters of the period were not concerned, when adorning buildings, in imposing the element of decoration on those of illustration, narrative or expression; and the Scalzo is perhaps a unique achievement in High Renaissance painting.

THE ART OF Leonardo and Michelangelo was at once the most splendid and the last of the great manifestations of Florentine culture, and history may regard it as dramatically fitting that this remarkable climax largely coincided with the greatest and also the final phase of Florentine republicanism.

With the accession of Charles V to the thrones both of Spain and the Holy Roman Empire, the chances of a French victory in the struggle for Italian dominion were fatally diminished; yet the Florentines continued, obstinately, to rely on the traditional connection with France and, in so doing, ensured the final destruction of their ancient if battered republican institutions. But, in defence of these, the citizens were able at last to show that the volatility of their democratic temper was not necessarily inconsistent with vigour and efficiency; and when their city was besieged by superior Imperial forces, they fought, though in vain, with a military competence and valour unprecedented in their history.

Andrea was a victim of the plague which followed the fall of the city and died from this cause in 1530 at the relatively youthful age of forty-four. His art had developed in the shadow of the triumphs of his great contemporaries; he had perforce followed with assiduity their example; that he did so with a consummate mechanical perfection was acknowledged at the time, though it was also perceived that this perfection was served by a somewhat fragile inspiration.

The study of Andrea's conceptions suggests the notion that he was a quattrocento master confronted with a world of ideas, the real meaning of which he was ill-equipped to grasp. The enduring merit of his art, which, notwithstanding the instability of his posthumous repute, has never been denied, may arise from the presence in it of a fifteenth-century realism and grace, pulsating beneath the polish and calculation of the classical convention.

3. STUDY FOR A HEAD OF 'CHARITY'. LOUVRE, PARIS

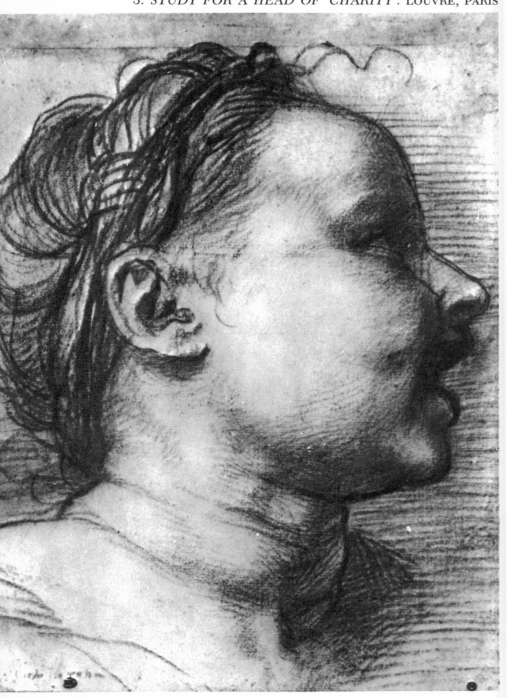

The Plates

I *STORIES FROM THE LIFE OF S. FILIPPO BENIZZI: THE DEATH OF THE SAINT AND THE LITTLE BOY BROUGHT BACK TO LIFE* C. 1510
Fresco. Detail.
SANTISSIMA ANNUNZIATA, FLORENCE

This illustrates Andrea's early style of about 1510 which was to some extent based on the classical style of Raphael. The figures are harmoniously grouped in a semi-circle round the bier so that they echo the lines of the architecture, and are painted with a restrained chiaroscuro.

II *STORIES FROM THE LIFE OF S. FILIPPO BENIZZI: THE PUNISHMENT OF THE GAMBLERS* C. 1510
Fresco. 144 in. × 121½ in.
SANTISSIMA ANNUNZIATA, FLORENCE

This way of illustrating the miracles of saints has some precedent in the great narrative fresco cycles of the late fifteenth century in the Florentine churches. The scene is made immediately recognisable by the use of expressive and natural details.

III *STORIES FROM THE LIFE OF S. FILIPPO BENIZZI: THE PUNISHMENT OF THE GAMBLERS* C. 1510
Fresco. Detail.
SANTISSIMA ANNUNZIATA, FLORENCE

This broad landscape is already far removed from the static calm of the classical landscapes and seems inspired by the restlessness associated with Mannerism. Little paths straggle up between the green hillocks crowned with spiky trees and clumps of bushes which cling precariously to the edge of the rocks.

IV *THE PROCESSION OF THE MAGI* 1511
Fresco. Detail.
SANTISSIMA ANNUNZIATA, FLORENCE

This is dated 1511. The landscape and also the milling crowd of the retinue, swathed in voluminous cloaks falling in rich folds, create a balanced classical rhythm, and yet foreshadow the Mannerist predilection for a more complex formal construction.

V *THE VIRGIN AND CHILD WITH ST. JOHN* C. 1516
Oil on canvas. 61½ in. × 40½ in.
GALLERIA BORGHESE, ROME

This picture, painted about 1516, shows the influence of Michelangelo in the lively movement of the two nude children and the plasticity of their bodies. The steep foreshortening of the Christ Child's face and the pointing arm of the young St. John emphasise this affinity, which is exceptional in Andrea's work.

VI-VII *THE BIRTH OF THE VIRGIN* 1514
Fresco. 165 in. × 138 in.
SANTISSIMA ANNUNZIATA, FLORENCE

This fresco, dated 1514, is one of Andrea's most admired works. It is a typical example of the traditional Florentine presentation of the subject, in a rich yet intimate setting. His pictorial idiom is now mature and shows a close study of works in Florence by Raphael, Leonardo and Michelangelo.

VIII *MADONNA OF THE HARPIES* 1517
Oil on canvas. Detail.
UFFIZI, FLORENCE

This work is dated 1517. It takes its name from the so-called 'harpies' on the corners of the hexagonal base on which the Virgin stands. There is already a suggestion of the revolutionary character of this composition in sketches by Fra Bartolommeo and Albertinelli, but Andrea articulates his figures more strongly against a dark background, using a subtle interplay of light and shadow.

7

IX *PORTRAIT OF A SCULPTOR*
C. 1517-18
Oil on canvas. 27½ in. × 22 in.
NATIONAL GALLERY, LONDON

It has been suggested that this is a portrait of Andrea's friend, Jacopo Sansovino, who was still in Florence in 1517-18, which seems on stylistic grounds to be a likely date for this picture. It shows an exceptionally fine use of colour, especially in the expressive contrast of greys.

X-XI *STORIES FROM THE LIFE OF JOSEPH* C. 1515
Oil on canvas. 38 in. × 54 in.
PALAZZO PITTI, FLORENCE

This is one of a series of panels depicting the biblical story of Joseph, painted by Andrea and other Florentine artists. The narrative unfolds against the fantasy hill landscape which seems to reflect the strange circumstances of the events. This panel depicts Joseph leaving the house of his father and the return of his brother.

XII *THE LAST SUPPER*
C. 1526-7
Fresco. Detail.
SAN SALVI, FLORENCE

This was commissioned when the painter was still young, but was not executed until much later in his life. It demonstrates his later extreme simplification of architectural forms, reflected also in the table. His technique is now entirely fluent but economical, and yet still flexible enough for each line to be expressive, as in the head of Christ.

XIII *PIETÀ* C. 1519-20
Oil on canvas. 40 in. × 48 in.
KUNSTHISTORISCHES MUSEUM, VIENNA

This is one of Andrea's most exciting works, not only in the realistic presentation and studied rhythm of the forms but also on account of the moving sincerity which infuses the isolated body of Christ and the silent agony on the drawn face of the Virgin, who is supported between the two angels.

XIV *THE DEPOSITION*
C. 1523
Oil on canvas. 95 in. × 79 in.
PALAZZO PITTI, FLORENCE

This was painted for the monastery of San Piero a Luco in the Mugello, where Andrea took refuge from the severe plague of 1523. It was inspired by the famous Pieta by Fra Bartolommeo, but Andrea's composition is far more coherent and evocative in the way he places figures in space and describes their piety and sorrow by their gestures and expressions.

XV *THE ASSUMPTION OF THE VIRGIN* C. 1526
Oil on canvas. 151½ in. × 100 in.
PALAZZO PITTI, FLORENCE

It is possible to argue that this was hastily executed on account of the dry, chalky appearance of the paint surface. But the whole conception of a double coronet of angels surrounding the ascending Virgin above, and of the majestic apostles round the tomb below, is impressive in its broad yet expressive simplicity.

XVI *THE SACRIFICE OF ISAAC* 1529
Oil on canvas. 93 in. × 63½ in.
GEMÄLDEGALERIE, DRESDEN

Modified copies of this work also exist in Madrid and Cleveland. The figure of Isaac has been related to one in the famous antique sculpture group, the Laocoön, which Andrea may have known from the little copy made by Bandinelli who was in Florence in 1524. The landscape is also very striking.

Cover Plate *THE VIRGIN AND CHILD WITH AN ANGEL AND A SAINT* C. 1522
(Copy from the lost original)
Oil on canvas. 71 in. × 54 in.
PRADO, MADRID

This is traditionally called the Madonna of the Steps. The artist has concentrated on the problem of a much tighter balance within the composition. The figures seem defined with the clarity of sculpture, their clean outlines revealed through his use of a more translucent play of light and shadow.

III

V

IX

XII

XIII